Editor

Eric Migliaccio

Editor in Chief

Ina Massler Levin, M.A.

Creative Director

Karen J. Goldfluss, M.S. Ed.

Cover Artist

Barb Lorseyedi

Art Coordinator

Renée Mc Elwee

Imaging

Rosa C. See

Publisher

Mary D. Smith, M.S. Ed.

Sep. 2013

D1399240

LEARNING TO

Print

GRADES K-2

Hh

hat

Tt

turtle

Ll

lion

Practice writing:
- individual letters
- letter combinations
- words
- complete sentences

Teacher Created Resources

Author

Teacher Created Resources Staff

Teacher Created Resources

6421 Industry Way
Westminster, CA 92683
www.teachercreated.com

ISBN: 978-1-4206-2769-5

© 2012 Teacher Created Resources
Made in U.S.A.

Teacher Created Resources

Table of Contents

Introduction

The activities in *Learning to Print* will help improve a student's ability to communicate through writing. Being able to write fluently is a skill all children need to learn. Printing helps improve students' fine motor skills and allows them a new way to express themselves on paper. Most students are excited about learning to print and cannot wait to practice. This is exactly what the activities in *Learning to Print* can provide.

Although much of the book is organized alphabetically, the pages in the book can be used in any order. One good way to start using the activities is to use the workbook pages that teach the letters in the child's name. All children enjoy seeing their own names in print, and this will also help lend excitement to learning other letters and words. Regardless of where you begin, both parents and teachers will find that children will enjoy the activities in *Learning to Print* while learning and practicing valuable skills.

Standards that are covered in *Learning to Print* include the following skills:

Uses grammatical and mechanical conventions in written compositions

- Uses conventions of print in writing

- Uses complete sentences in written compositions

- Uses conventions of spelling in written compositions

- Uses conventions of capitalization in written compositions

- Uses conventions of punctuation in written compositions

Name _____

Printing Practice for Aa

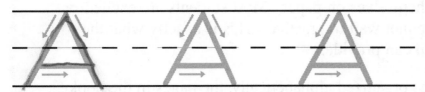

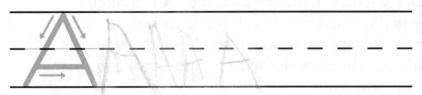

apple

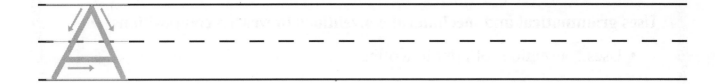

Word Practice for Aa

apple

and

ant

I have an apple.

Name _____

Printing Practice for Bb

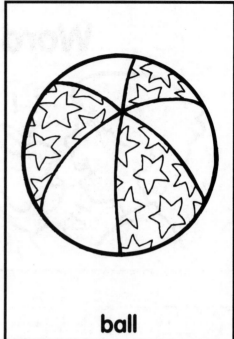

ball

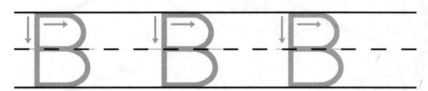

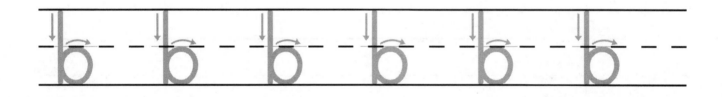

Word Practice for Bb

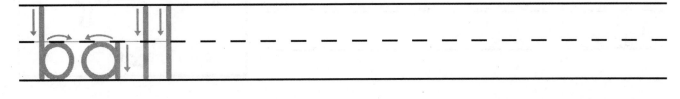

ball

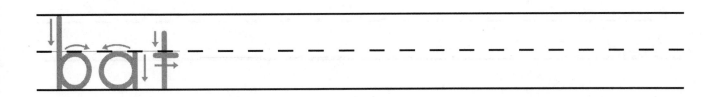

bat

boy

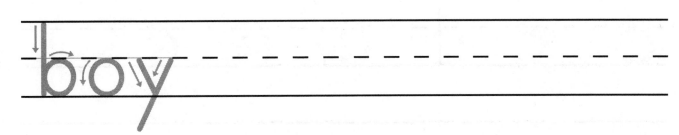

I have a ball.

Printing Practice for Cc

cat

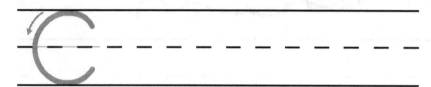

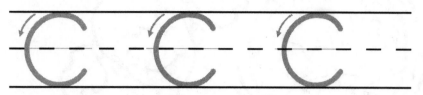

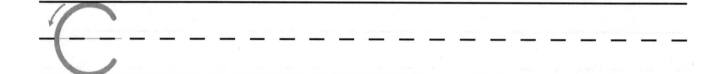

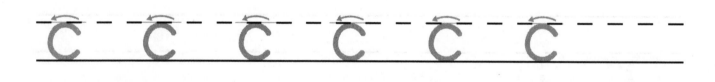

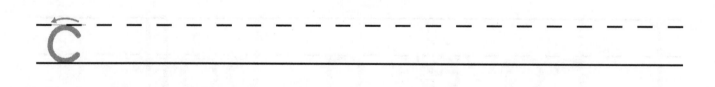

Word Practice for Cc

cat

car

come

I see the big cat.

Printing Practice for D d

dog

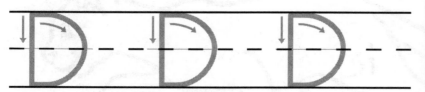

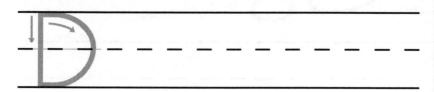

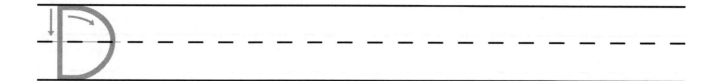

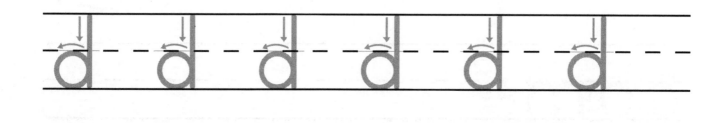

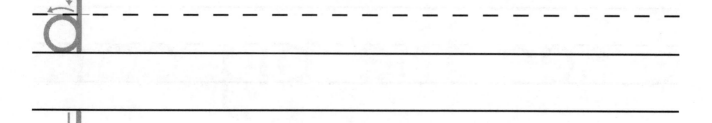

Word Practice for Dd

dog

dad

duck

A dog met a duck.

Printing Practice for Ee

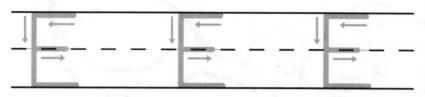

elephant

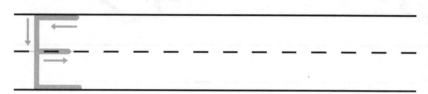

E   E   E

E

E

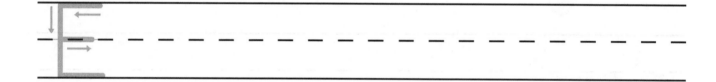

e   e   e   e   e   e

e

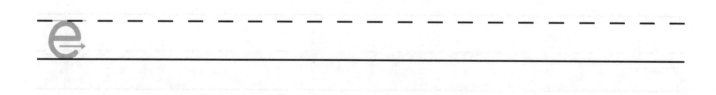

e

Word Practice for Ee

elephant

egg

elf

The elf is small.

Name _____

Printing Practice for Ff

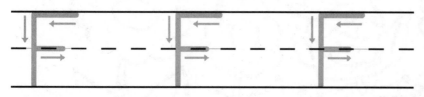

fish

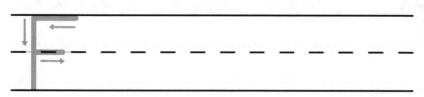

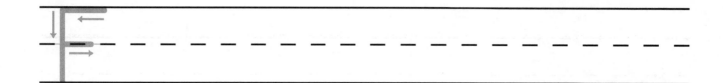

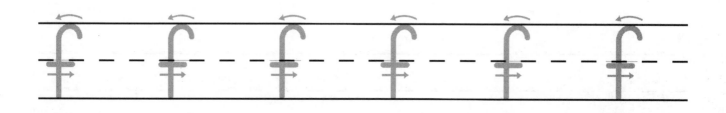

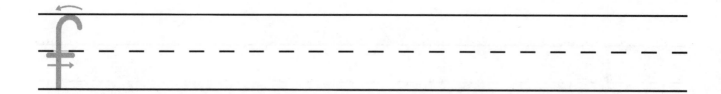

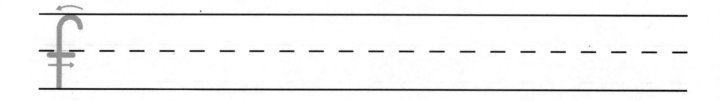

Word Practice for Ff

fish

fast

fun

A fish swims fast.

Name
Name _____

Printing Practice for G g

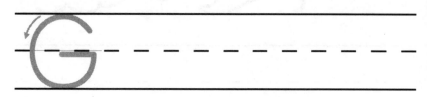

girl

Word Practice for Gg

girl

get

go

Go get the girl.

Printing Practice for Hh

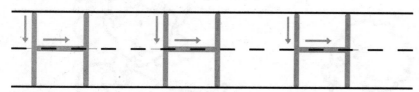

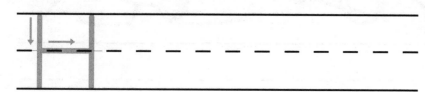

hat

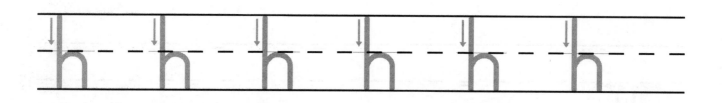

Word Practice for Hh

hat

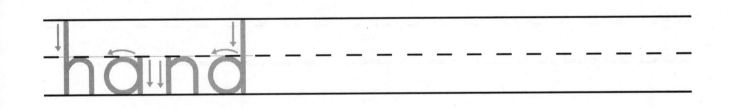
hand

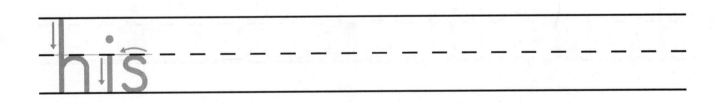
his

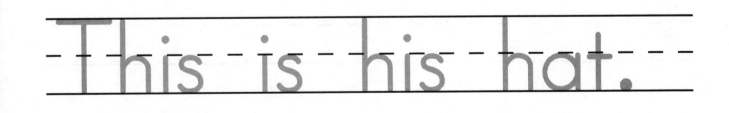
This is his hat.

Name _____

Printing Practice for Ii

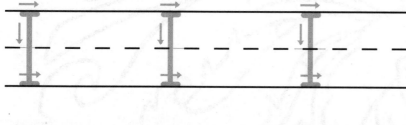

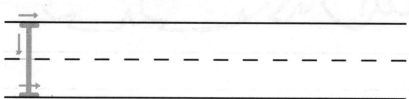

insect

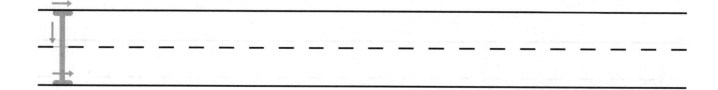

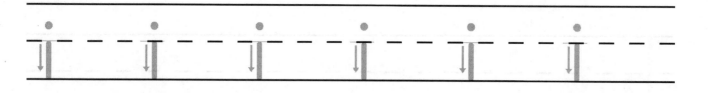

Name _____

Word Practice for Ii

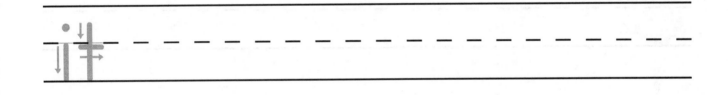

insect

it

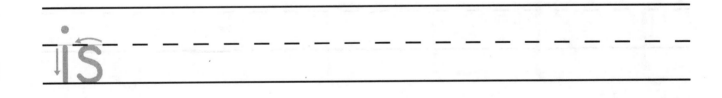

is

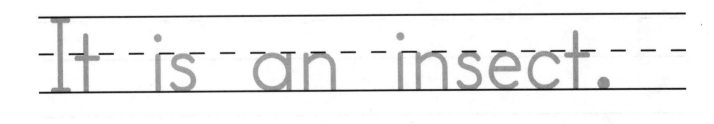

It is an insect.

Printing Practice for Jj

jar

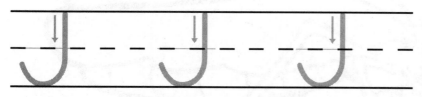

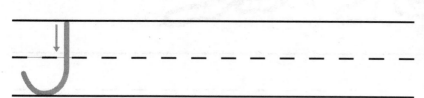

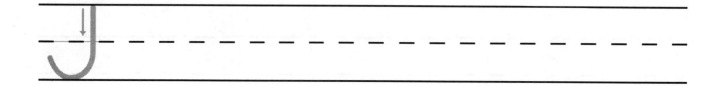

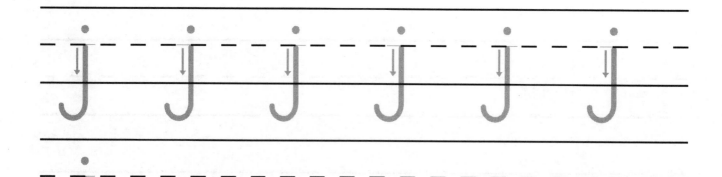

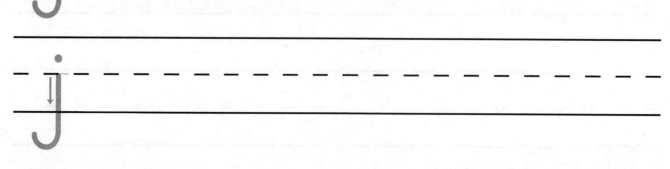

Word Practice for Jj

jar

jump

jelly

Jack jumps high.

Printing Practice for Kk

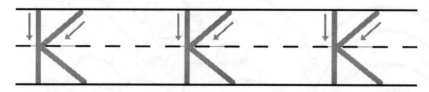

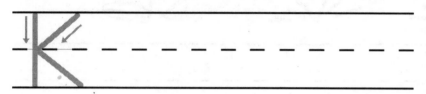

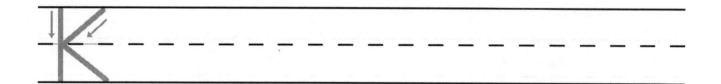

kite

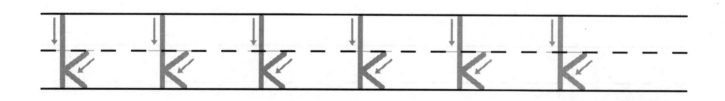

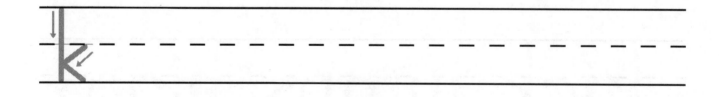

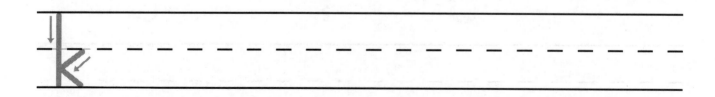

Word Practice for Kk

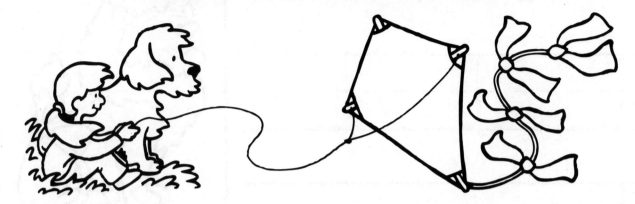

kite

kick

kiss

We will fly a kite.

Printing Practice for Ll

lion

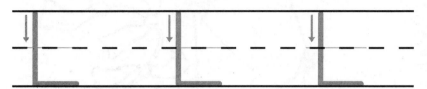

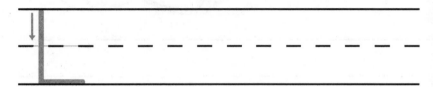

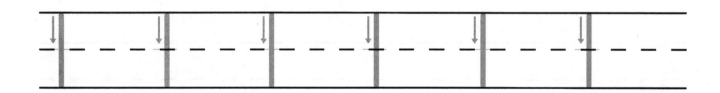

Word Practice for Ll

lion

look

like

I like two lions.

Printing Practice for Mm

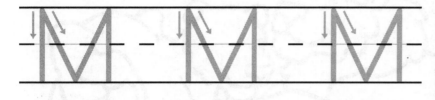

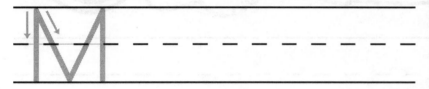

mouse

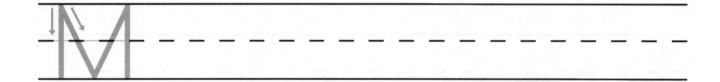

Word Practice for Mm

mouse

mom

my

She saw the moon.

Name _____

Printing Practice for Nn

nest

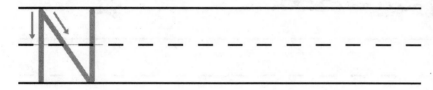

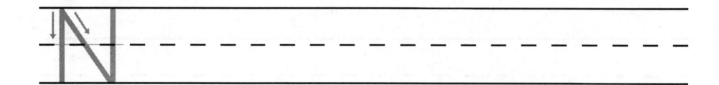

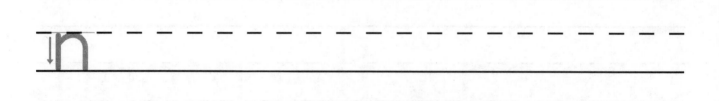

Name _____

Word Practice for Nn

nest

no

not

That is a nest.

Printing Practice for Oo

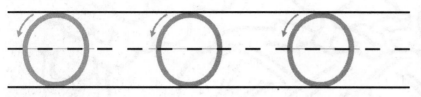

octopus

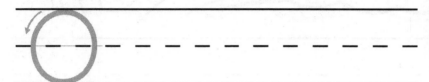

Name _____

Word Practice for Oo

octopus

on

our

I see an octopus.

Printing Practice for Pp

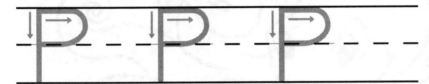

pig

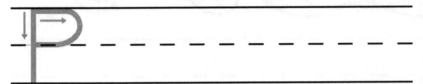

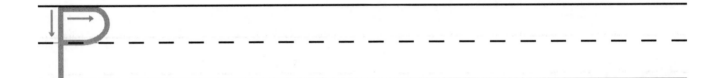

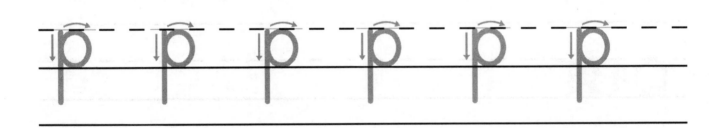

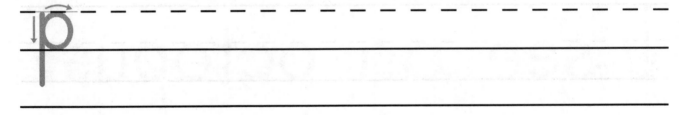

Word Practice for Pp

pig

play

pen

The pig plays.

Name _____

Printing Practice for Qq

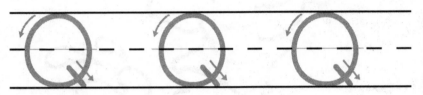

queen

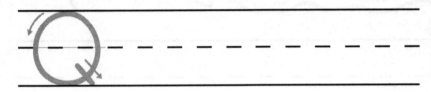

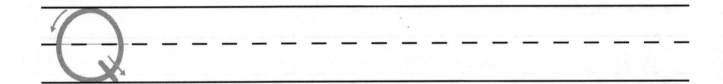

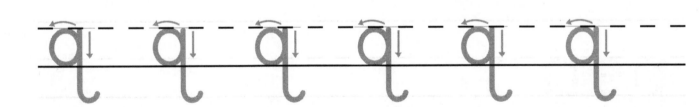

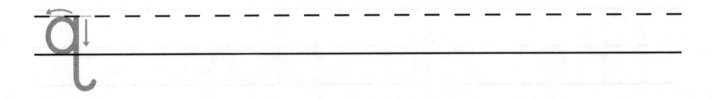

Name _____

Word Practice for Qq

queen

quilt

quack

A duck quacks.

Printing Practice for Rr

rabbit

Word Practice for Rr

rabbit

ride

run

Rabbits can run.

Name _____

Printing Practice for Ss

sun

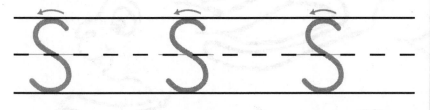

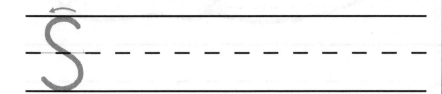

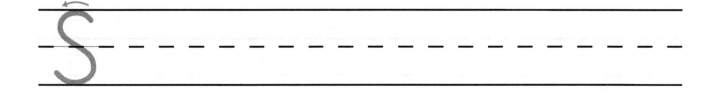

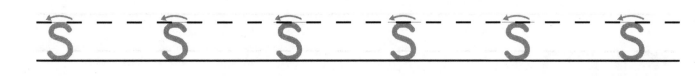

Word Practice for Ss

sun

star

stop

We see the sun.

Printing Practice for Tt

turtle

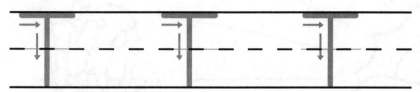

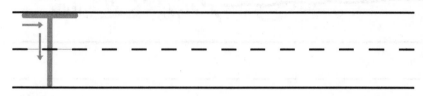

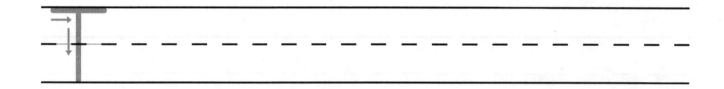

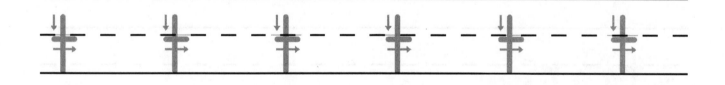

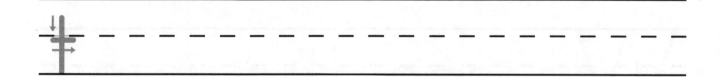

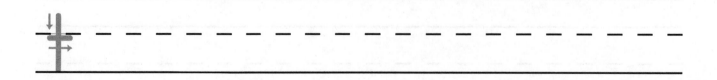

Word Practice for Tt

turtle

teeth

tree

I see a big turtle.

Printing Practice for Uu

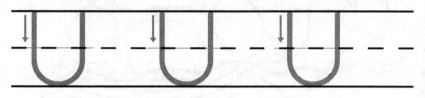

umbrella

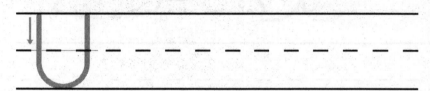

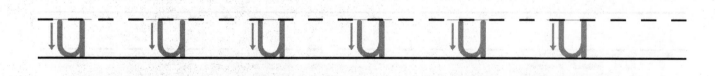

Name _____

Word Practice for Uu

umbrella

up

under

The umbrella is up.

Printing Practice for Vv

valentine

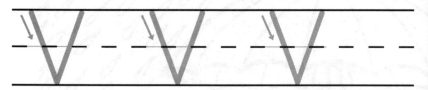

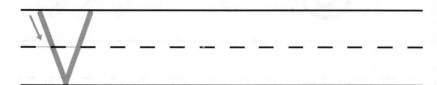

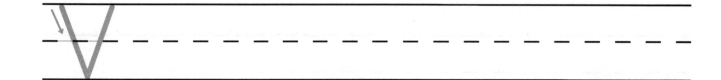

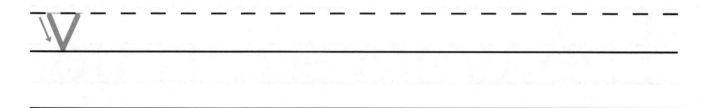

Word Practice for Vv

valentine

vegetable

vet

I eat vegetables.

Printing Practice for Ww

watermelon

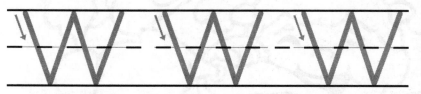

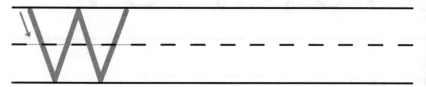

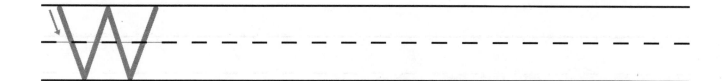

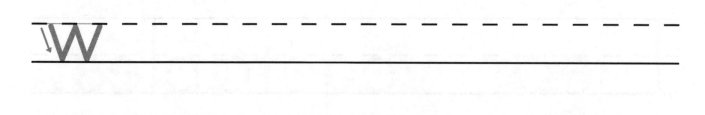

48

Word Practice for Ww

watermelon

wall

web

I like watermelon.

Printing Practice for Xx

box

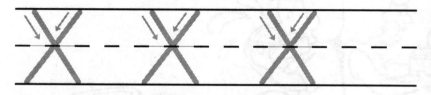

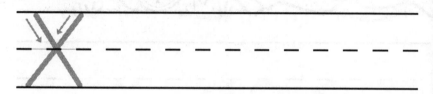

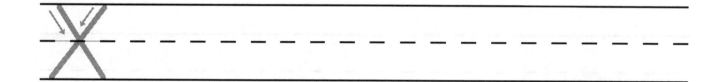

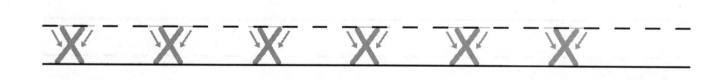

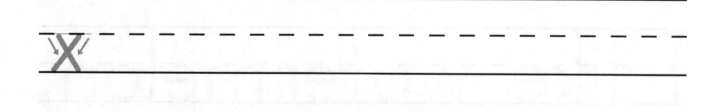

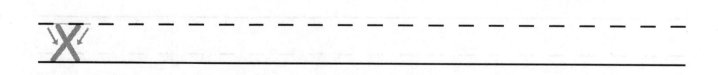

Name _____

Word Practice for Xx

box

fox

six

A fox is in a box.

Printing Practice for Yy

yarn

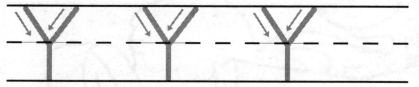

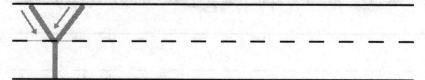

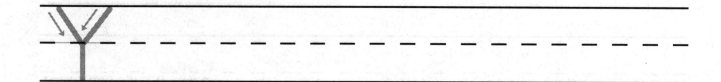

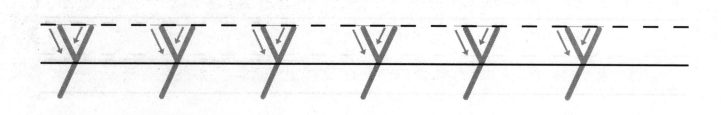

Word Practice for Yy

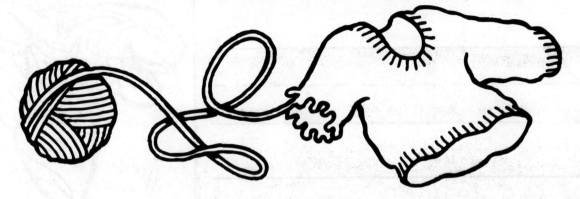

yarn

yard

yes

I see the yarn.

Printing Practice for Zz

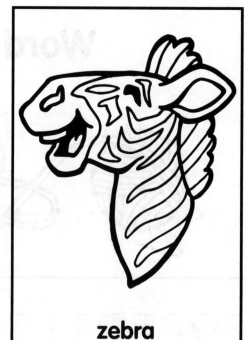

zebra

54

Word Practice for Zz

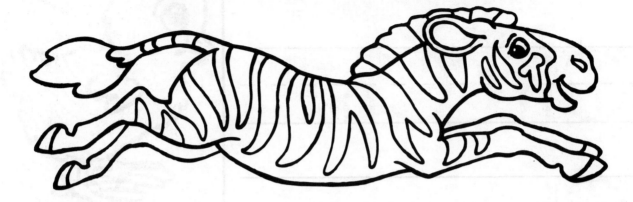

zebra

zipper

zoo

I see the zebra.

Printing Practice for Ch

chick

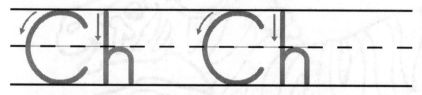

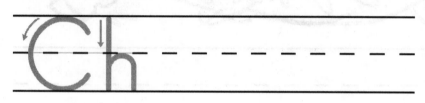

Ch

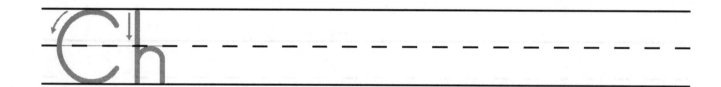

ch

ch

Word Practice for Ch

chick

chair

chill

I see a chick.

Printing Practice for Sh

Sh Sh

Sh

Sh

ship

sh sh sh sh sh sh sh sh sh sh

sh

sh

Name _____

Word Practice for Sh

ship

sheep

shop

We see a ship.

Name _____

Printing Practice for Wh

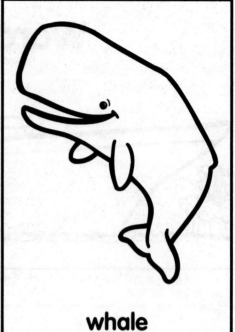

whale

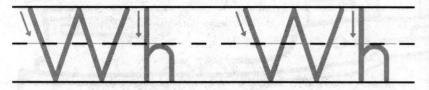

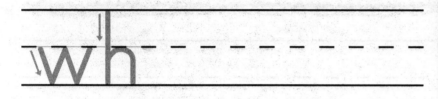

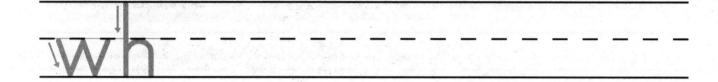

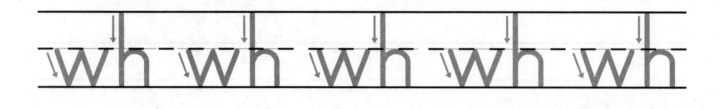

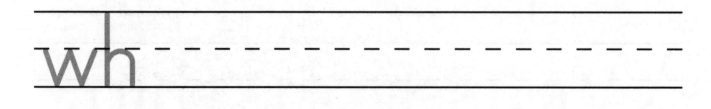

wh

wh

Word Practice for Wh

whale

wheel

white

The whale swims.

Name _____

Lowercase Alphabet

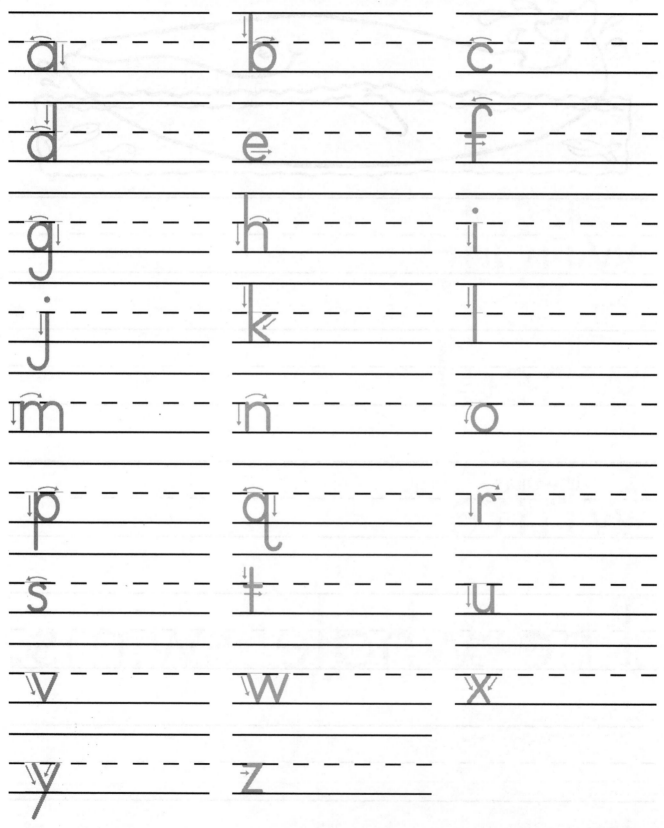

Uppercase Alphabet

A B C

D E F

G H I

J K L

M N O

P Q R

S T U

V W X

Y Z

Name _____

Printing Practice